CURRICTER

D1450335

★ IN THE FOOTSTEPS OF AMERICAN HEROES ★

LEWIS AND CLARK
on Their Journey to the Pacific

Richard Sapp

WORLD ALMANAC® LIBRARY

Please visit our web site at: www.worldalmanaclibrary.com
For a free color catalog describing World Almanac® Library's list of high-quality books
and multimedia programs, call 1-800-848-2928 (USA) or 1-800-387-3178 (Canada).
World Almanac® Library's fax: (414) 332-3567.

Library of Congress Cataloging-in-Publication Data

Sapp, Richard.
    Lewis and Clark on their journey to the Pacific / Richard Sapp.
        p. cm. — (In the footsteps of American heroes)
    Includes bibliographical references and index.
    ISBN 0-8368-6429-8 (lib. bdg.)
    ISBN 0-8368-6434-4 (softcover)
        1. Lewis and Clark Expedition (1804-1806)—Juvenile literature.
    2. Lewis, Meriwether, 1774-1809—Juvenile literature. 3. Clark, William,
    1770-1838—Juvenile literature. 4. Explorers—West (U.S.)—Biography—
    Juvenile literature. 5. West (U.S.)—Discovery and exploration—Juvenile literature.
    6. West (U.S.)—Description and travel—Juvenile literature. I. Title. II. Series.
    F592.7S12443   2006
    917.804'2—dc22   2005054473

First published in 2006 by
World Almanac® Library
A Member of the WRC Media Family of Companies
330 West Olive Street, Suite 100
Milwaukee, WI 53212 USA

Produced by Compendium Publishing Ltd
First Floor, 43 Frith Street
London W1D 4SA

For Compendium Publishing
Editors: Don Gulbrandsen and Joe Hollander
Picture research: Mindy Day and Sandra Forty
Design: Ian Hughes/Compendium Design
Artwork: Mark Franklin

World Almanac® Library managing editor: Valerie J. Weber
World Almanac® Library editor: Leifa Butrick
World Almanac® Library art direction: Tammy West
World Almanac® Library production: Jessica Morris and Robert Kraus

Photo Credits: CORBIS: cover pages, 1, 4, 7, 12(both), 15(b), 19, 20(t), 21(b), 22, 26–31, 33(t),
34(t), 35, 37–41, 42(t), 43, 47, 48–52; Library of Congress: page 8; Getty Images: 5, 9, 11, 13, 15(t),
16, 17, 20(B), 21(t), 23, 33(b), 34(b), 36, 42(b), 44, 45, 56, 57(both)

Printed in the United States of America

1 2 3 4 5 6 7 8 9 10 09 08 07 06

CONTENTS

COVER: **This memorial statue of William Clark, Meriwether Lewis, and Sacagawea by Bob Scriver stands next to the Missouri River. Their work exploring the Louisiana Purchase helped change the shape of their country.**

TITLE PAGE: **This sculpture, entitled *End of the Trail* by Stanley Wanlass, marks Lewis and Clark's expedition's arrival on the Pacific coast.**

INTRODUCTION

T wo hundred years ago, a small band of explorers left home and traveled thousands of miles across an unknown land. They had no maps of the land ahead of them and no friends along the way. They could not carry all the food they would need, and they expected to encounter fierce and warlike people. When they arrived at their destination, they would almost certainly have to turn around . . . and return by the same path.

The explorers did not know what dangers they might face, what hardships they would encounter, or what discoveries they might make. Some expected to find mammoths or other strange, fierce animals. Others dreamed of finding a shortcut—called the Northwest Passage—a water route to the Pacific Ocean and hence to the silks, spices, and other goods of the Far East.

There were no mammoths, there were no quick fortunes to be made, and there was no easy way. Instead, the explorers worked very hard every day for two and one-half

years. In the heat of summer, they paddled heavy canoes upstream against the rushing current of wild rivers. They smeared their skin with bear grease to discourage hordes of mosquitoes. When temperatures fell to 42 degrees below zero Farenheit (-23.5 degrees Celsius), their fingers and toes suffered from frostbite. They scrambled over trackless mountains. Days passed when there was nothing to eat. Their nation gave them up for dead. When they arrived at their destination, it proved so disappointing that some of them wanted to return home immediately.

In spite of the difficult conditions, the explorers believed in themselves and their captains. They got lost and they got lucky, but no one got rich. Some of them became national heroes, but most were soon forgotten. The explorers discovered plants, fish, birds, and animals unknown to their nation. They made contact with peoples who had never before met outsiders. They made detailed maps so that others could follow, and they kept careful journals detailing what they saw and providing an important

The main locations mentioned in the text are featured on this map with present-day state boundaries shown. The numbers identify sites related to Lewis and Clark that are detailed in the Places to Visit and Research section of this book on page 58–59. The green dots represent sites that are discussed in the sidebars. The red dots represent other sites connected to Lewis and Clark's journey.

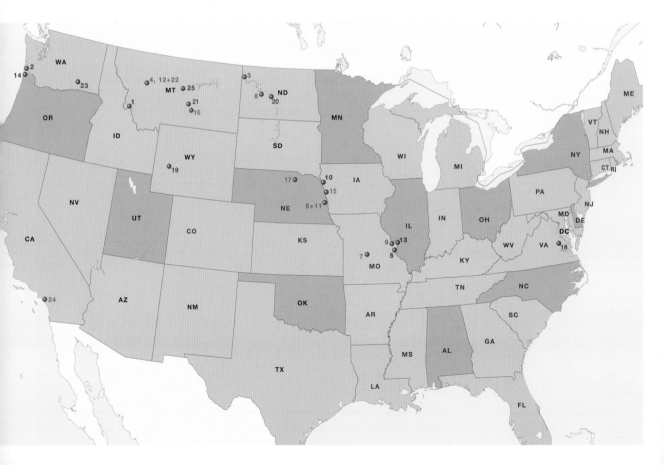

resource for discovering what life was like in the early days of our country. They were trailblazers who proved that immense prairies, rugged mountains, and imagined terrors were not barriers, only challenges to the mind and body. They proved that the United States' newly acquired territory to the west was a land of opportunity—one that would beckon new settlers for the next century.

These explorers were Meriwether Lewis, William Clark, and the Corps of Discovery, the group of people that President Thomas Jefferson had told Lewis and Clark to assemble to help on their journey. Today, two hundred years after their epic expedition, it is easy to see just how inspiring their efforts were to a young country trying to establish itself on the world stage.

A Lewis and Clark trail marker on U.S. Highway 12

CHAPTER 1

AT THE REQUEST OF THE PRESIDENT

Thomas Jefferson was an influential Virginian—a well-to-do lawyer who owned a plantation. One of an elite group of men who guided Britain's American colonies through the Revolutionary War, Jefferson penned the first draft of the Declaration of Independence in 1776 when he was only thirty-three years old. He was elected governor of Virginia and became the third president of the young republic.

Jefferson was far ahead of the thinking—if not always of the actions—of his time. He argued for religious freedom before that was a popular idea. Fellow politicians scorned his proposals for public libraries and public schools. Jefferson believed in the universal rights of man, although he himself owned slaves. A farmer and scientist, Jefferson raised traditional crops that exhausted the soil (tobacco and cotton), but he promoted contour plowing (which protected the soil) and experimented with new plant varieties. A spellbinding writer, the tall redhead was a poor public speaker. As president, he peacefully doubled the size of the United

Thomas Jefferson was the third president of the United States and was in office from 1801 until 1809.

Thomas Jefferson's study at Monticello features a polygraph on his desk. This machine enabled the making of copies of handwritten letters. By 1804 Jefferson used his polygraph machine (he always updated to the latest model) exclusively for duplicating his correspondence.

States, but he was not certain he had the authority to do so under the Constitution.

Jefferson was a firm believer that farming was a vital part of the economy of the young country, so it is not surprising that he bought 828,000 square miles (2.14 million square kilometers) of land from France. Americans in rural areas required farms to raise everything they needed to survive—food, clothing, and shelter—plus crops to sell for things they could not grow or make. In the South, most plantations cultivated tobacco and cotton for export. These labor-intensive crops relied on the hard work of slaves and on abundant land. Because crop rotation and fertilizer were practically unheard of, eighteenth-century farming practices quickly exhausted the soil. New lands thus meant new soil for farming.

Jefferson was interested in the lands west of the

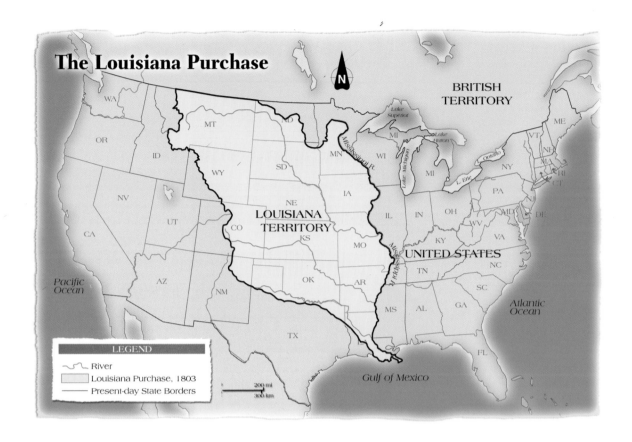

The Louisiana Purchase

BRITISH TERRITORY

LOUISIANA TERRITORY

UNITED STATES

Pacific Ocean

Atlantic Ocean

Gulf of Mexico

LEGEND
River
Louisiana Purchase, 1803
Present-day State Borders

200 mi
300 km

In 1801, Thomas Jefferson sent an ambassador to France to negotiate the purchase of New Orleans from Emperor Napoleon Bonaparte. After considerable bargaining, Napoleon agreed to sell the Louisiana Territory to the United States in 1803 for about $15 million.

Mississippi River long before the United States bought them. Following the Revolutionary War, he discussed western exploration with war hero (and brother of William Clark) George Rogers Clark, but nothing came of it.

When Jefferson became president in 1801, Britain and France were both important trading partners for the United States, but the two countries were actively hostile to each another. Although two-thirds of U.S. citizens lived within 50 miles (80 kilometers) of the Atlantic coast in those days, migration over the Appalachian Mountains and down the Ohio River to the Mississippi had begun in earnest. Each year, U.S. citizens shipped larger cargoes of farm products and beaver pelts through the French port of New Orleans. If Britain and France went to war, that port might close, which would hurt western commerce.

When Thomas Jefferson became president, he was still interested in the land west of the United States. He directed Robert Livingston, his ambassador to France, to discuss the purchase of New Orleans with French emperor Napoleon. At the very least, the president wanted a guarantee that the United States could freely transport cargo on the Mississippi River.

France was at war with its neighbors and in a difficult position. Napoleon had dreamed of a New World empire based on the sugar trade, but those dreams were fading. Instead, Napoleon was focusing his attention on controlling Europe, and he had started stockpiling money for the war he was planning.

Negotiator Pierre Samuel du Pont de Nemours was the first person to suggest that France sell all of its Louisiana territory to the United States. Napoleon was not initially interested, but he was concerned about how the United States might affect his plans in Europe. Napoleon soon realized that selling Louisiana might help keep the United States as a strong ally against their mutual enemy, the

James Monroe (1758–1831), who would go on to become the fifth president of the United States, and Robert R. Livingstone (1746–1813) completing negotiations with Comte Talleyrand (1754–1838) for the Louisiana Purchase.

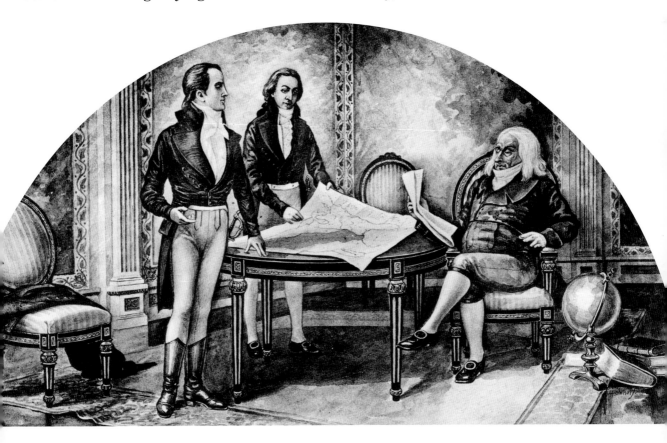

Right: Portrait of Thomas Jefferson, circa 1791, by **Charles Willson Peale (1741–1827)**

British. President Jefferson sent James Monroe to negotiate the final purchase. In April 1803, Napoleon offered New Orleans and all of the land to the west for $15 million. In the end, the United States government paid $11.25 million cash and assumed its citizens' claims against France, which amounted to $3.75 million. The purchase meant that America doubled in size for about 3¢ per acre. Jefferson was concerned that the purchase might not be legal according to the Constitution, and that Napoleon might change his mind. He also might have wondered what right the French had to sell land lived on by Indians for generations, or what right his own new country had to buy it. No one knows if these questions occurred to Jefferson, since the rights of the Native inhabitants of the new country were usually not of great concern to people at the time. In any event, Jefferson quickly submitted the treaty to the Senate, and the Senate overwhelmingly ratified the purchase.

Below: The Louisiana Purchase Treaty document

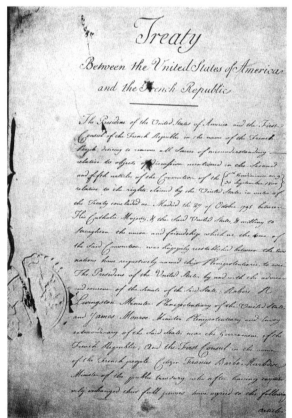

Meanwhile, Jefferson had already set in motion a plan to explore the territory west of the Mississippi. The ideal man to lead

BEAVER PELTS AND MOUNTAIN MEN

For more than three hundred years, men of consequence in Europe and the Americas wore felt hats made from beaver fur. One adult beaver pelt produced roughly enough material for one hat. A beaver felt hat was a prized and expensive possession. Consequently, beaver had been trapped to extinction in Europe and, by 1800, were difficult to find even in the vast wilderness of Siberia in Russia. One of the results of the Lewis and Clark expedition was opening the vast territory of the Louisiana Purchase to beaver trapping. In fact, one member of the Corps, John Colter, decided not to return with the party to St. Louis. He stayed in the Rocky Mountains trapping beaver, and thus he became one of the first "mountain men" who made their living off the land in this wild, beautiful country. Today the Museum of the Mountain Man in Pinedale, Wyoming (map reference 19), preserves the history of the nineteenth-century fur trade. The museum's annual rendezvous in July recreates the spirited gatherings when trappers, traders, and Native Americans came together to barter pelts and socialize.

One of the most important points of contact between settlers and Native Americans was through the fur trade. Beaver pelts, in particular, were prized.

such an expedition, he decided, was his friend, personal secretary, and fellow Virginian Meriwether Lewis. In 1802, Jefferson proposed the idea to Lewis, and the twenty-eight-year-old enthusiastically accepted.

CHAPTER 2

MERIWETHER, THOMAS, AND WILLIAM

Jefferson liked and trusted the young Lewis. Indeed, because Jefferson was a poor public speaker, he had even asked Lewis to deliver his State of the Union address.

Born in Virgnia, Meriwether Lewis grew up with one foot in society and the other firmly planted in the woods. His father, a planter and Revolutionary War officer, died when Lewis was only five years old. His mother then married another Revolutionary War officer, John Marks, who moved the family to Georgia. There, Lewis roamed the woods barefoot, hunting, fishing, and exploring. At thirteen, he returned alone to Virginia. Lewis needed an education, and his 2,000-acre (809-hectare) family farm there, Locust Hill, needed attention.

Obviously, Lewis was mature for his age. He was six feet tall, and friends described him as slender, serious, and moody. Just five years after his return to Virginia, Captain Marks died, and Lewis brought his family back to Locust Hill.

While running the family farm, Lewis studied with a tutor. He read the journals of British explorer Captain James Cook, which were filled with stories of strange lands and peoples. Cook wrote that he "had ambition, not only to go farther than anyone had been before, but as far as it was possible for man to go." By comparison, farming did not seem very exciting to Lewis, so he joined the militia. He soon earned a promotion to captain in the army and, for a time, served under William Clark, who became a close friend.

In 1801, Thomas Jefferson invited Captain Lewis to serve as his personal secretary. You will be treated "as one of my family," Jefferson wrote. Lewis was surprised by this

Opposite: **A bust of William Clark by William Ordway Partridge placed at Clark's grave in Bellefontaine Cemetery, St. Louis, Missouri**

WILLIAM CLARK

When William Clark agreed to join his friend Meriwether Lewis as part of the Corps of Discovery, he probably did not realize that the adventure would lead to his becoming one of America's greatest heroes. Clark's exploits with the Corps launched a successful career in public service. He was appointed the first governor of Missouri Territory in 1813, a post he held until the territory became a state in 1821. He later served a long tenure as the government's superintendent of Indian affairs for the West. He died in St. Louis in 1838 at the age of sixty-nine and was memorialized with a long funeral procession. In 1850, his body was moved to St. Louis's Bellefontaine Cemetery. The grave features a lavish monument, including a bronze bust of Clark and a tall stone obelisk.

William Clark

opportunity but replied that he would "with pleasure accept the office."

Jefferson was impressed with the young captain and soon selected Lewis to command an expedition to the West. Jefferson was interested in everything, and the president's library at Monticello contained the most up-to-date books and maps. The two men discussed the exploration in detail. Because this expedition was traveling into uncharted, possibly dangerous territory, and because it was going to be functioning without any support from the United States, Lewis needed to be trained to handle any problem he might encounter. It was also a scientific expedition, so Lewis also needed training in special subjects. Jefferson sent Lewis to Philadelphia to be tutored by the best men in their fields: Benjamin Rush for medicine, Andrew Ellicott for astronomy and celestial navigation, and Benjamin Smith Barton for botanical identification and description.

Jefferson was greatly impressed by Meriwether Lewis when he worked as his private secretary. He chose him to lead the expedition to the West.

As Jefferson and Lewis pored over maps and developed lists of supplies, they realized the expedition needed more than one man and that Lewis needed another officer. On June 19, 1803, Lewis wrote army pal William Clark, inviting him to join the expedition and share "its dangers and its honors." He said, "There is no man on earth with whom I should feel equal pleasure in sharing them as with yourself." Clark answered right away: "This is an undertaking fraught with many difficulties . . . . I join you with hand and heart."

Originally a Virginian, Clark was the ninth of ten children. After the American Revolution, his family emigrated to Kentucky, where they built a log cabin and eventually acquired 9,000 acres (3,642 hectares) of farmland and timber. They called their home Mulberry Hill, and it was there that Clark's brothers, who had fought the British and the Indians, taught him to read and write. When he was old enough to join the army, his older brothers were already heroes.

William Clark was both like Lewis and different. Where Lewis was studious and reclusive, the redheaded Clark was talkative and outgoing. Both men, however, were at home in the outdoors. They were natural leaders, quick thinking and courageous in adverse situations, and anxious for an adventure of their own.

Lewis offered Clark equal leadership of the expedition. The veteran army officers knew this was an unusual way to organize an expedition. The military was built on a clear chain of command that always led to a single leader for every group. This two-commander system, however, worked well, perhaps because the two men had a mutual respect for one another. For the next three years, it was not once reported that Lewis and Clark were ever in conflict.

Captain Meriwether Lewis and William Clark hold a council with Native Americans of the Omaha and Oto tribes at Council Bluffs, Iowa. This engraving is from the *Journal of the Voyages and Travels of a Corps of Discovery* (shortened to *Journal of Voyages*) by Patrick Gass, published in 1811.

CHAPTER 3
PREPARATIONS

In a secret communication on January 18, 1803—the land to be explored still belonged to France—Jefferson asked Congress to authorize a Corps of Discovery to investigate the territories west of the United States. He carefully emphasized its commercial potential and asked for only $2,500. (The final cost of the mission came to about $38,000.)

The president also labored over his written instructions to Lewis. He wrote, "The object of your mission is to explore the Missouri river, & such principal stream of it, as, by it's course & communication with the waters of the pacific Ocean, may offer the most direct & practicable water communication across this continent, for the purposes of commerce." Simply put, this meant that he thought the primary purpose of the mission was to travel up the Missouri River and find the fabled Northwest Passage water route to the Pacific Ocean.

The United States' purchase of the Louisiana Territories was announced on the fourth of July in 1803. The next day, Lewis left Monticello. At the Harper's Ferry arsenal, he ordered muskets. In Pittsburgh, he began construction of a keelboat to carry the Corps's supplies.

Lewis assembled more than two tons (1.8 metric tons) of supplies. In addition, his Philadelphia tutors loaned him scientific equipment: compasses, quadrants (for measuring altitude), telescopes, and chronometers (very accurate devices for measuring time). Lewis purchased a variety of items as gifts for the Native Americans: mirrors, combs, colorful ribbons, needles and thread, kettles, tobacco, knives, beads, bright cloth, handkerchiefs, face paint, and official certificates of greeting.

It was hard to know exactly what the Corps needed to bring. For example, Lewis realized that if a U. S. ship happened to appear at the mouth of the Columbia River while the Corps was present, the men could sail home. The area had been regularly visited by trading vessels since 1792, when Boston sea captain Robert Gray became the first white man to report viewing the Columbia River, which he named after his ship, the *Columbia*. Gray's accurate notes of latitude and longitude allowed geographers to pinpoint the river's mouth. Thus, they knew the continent was 3,000 miles (4,800 kilometers) wide, and Lewis and Clark knew how far they had to travel and where they must direct the expedition.

In the end, Lewis purchased soap, camping and medical supplies, weapons, and clothing. He also stocked up on food supplies: three bushels of salt, 50 kegs of salt pork, barrels of grease, 193 pounds (88 kilograms) of dried "portable soup," boiled beef, eggs, and vegetables. They packed writing supplies and portable desks, reference books, and tables for determining latitude and longitude to locate their position as they traveled.

Two unique items rounded out the cargo. The first was a remarkably unsuccessful 176-pound (80-kilogram),

The bow of a replica *Discovery* jut out of the Lewis and Clark National Historic Trail Interpretive Center (map reference 12).

collapsible iron-frame boat designed to float almost 8,000 total pounds (3,700 kilograms) of cargo. Lewis spent weeks on this pet project. He thought it would be useful on the difficult upper stretches of the Missouri River. He planned to stretch stitched animal skins around the frame. When the boat was eventually put together in Montana, it quickly sank because no suitable material was available to seal the seams where the skins overlapped.

Lewis's second innovation was a .31-caliber air rifle. Although it was powerful enough to kill a deer, the air rifle fired silently without emitting the telltale smoke that marked blackpowder muskets. Unfortunately, the rifle's performance was inconsistent, and Lewis relegated it to carefully arranged ceremonial occasions.

Meanwhile, Clark interviewed prospective Corps members. He rejected gentlemen and professionals in favor of soldiers, hunters, and men who spoke Native American languages. The expedition needed men who could live in the outdoors and give up the comforts of home.

Finally, the president had commemorative copper coins minted. Called Jefferson Peace Medals, they were presents Lewis would give to Indian leaders as tokens of peace and friendship.

An illustration from the *Journal of Voyages*. It shows Lewis and Clark hunting.

The Permanent Party

In addition to Lewis and Clark, the permanent party of the Corps of Discovery consisted of thirty-one men who made the trip from the Mississippi to the Pacific and then returned. Clark's slave York also made that round trip,

apparently working as hard and contributing as much as any other member, although he was not paid. Numerous skilled individuals, who worked as guides, interpreters, and hunters, joined and left the Corps during its journey.

Seaman, Lewis's "dogg of the Newfoundland breed" also accompanied him. (Note: This book contains many excerpts from the *Journals of Lewis and Clark*, and several have words that are strangely spelled, such as

Above: Hunter Hugh McNeal takes refuge in the branches of a tree after a close encounter with a grizzly bear. He was a member of the expedition. From the *Journal of Voyages.*

Left: Reenactors portray Meriwether Lewis and William Clark during Lewis and Clark Heritage Days in St. Charles, Missouri. Note how the uniforms and hats match the engraving on the opposite page.

21

In commemoration of the Louisiana Purchase and Lewis and Clark's expedition, the United States Mint unveiled a redesigned nickel (five-cent coin) in November 6, 2003. The design featured a side-view of the Lewis and Clark keelboat that transported members of the expedition and their supplies. It was possible to sail, row, pole, or tow the 55-foot (17-meter) keelboat along a riverbank. The design, by United States Mint sculptor/engraver Al Maletsky, shows Captains Lewis and Clark in full uniform in the bow of the keelboat.

Opposite: A canoe carrying two men across a river strikes a tree and overturns during the expedition. From the *Journal of Voyages.*

"dogg" instead of "dog." Both Lewis and Clark were educated and good writers, but at the time of the expedition, rules for spelling and punctuation did not exist as they do today. Writers were free to choose their own spelling of a word.

Two men, privates Moses Reed and John Newman, were dismissed from the permanent party early in the journey. Reed was convicted of desertion and Newman of "mutinous acts." Severe punishments for these crimes were imposed in trials by court martial, but because the Corps was traveling through a wilderness, both men remained with the party during the first winter, performing the hardest labor the captains could impose. In the spring of 1805, when the rest of the Corps headed west, Reed and Newman were sent back to St. Louis aboard the keelboat.

PUNISHMENT IN THE CORPS OF DISCOVERY

Moses Reed's offense was desertion from the Corps of Discovery. On August 3, 1804, Reed told the captains that he had left his knife at the site of a council with Indian tribes earlier in the day. They gave him permission to retrieve it. When he failed to return, a search party was organized. It was authorized to shoot Reed if he did not come back willingly. When he was captured, Reed confessed that he took a rifle and other Corps supplies. A court martial sentenced him to run the gauntlet four times and to be dismissed from the Corps.

Running the gauntlet required a man to dash between two lines of men who would hit him with a fistful of nine switches. He received a punishment of about five hundred lashes on his bare back. The captains could order a man shot for desertion, so this was considered a lenient punishment.

Although he was dismissed from the Corps, Reed remained and worked until the spring of 1805. When the others headed west, he returned with the keelboat from Fort Mandan.

Reed's bad attitude infected John Newman, who whispered about the captains and suggested others might rebel (mutiny) against them. Newman received seventy-five lashes on his bare back. In spite of excellent behavior thereafter, he, too, was dismissed from the Corps and returned with the keelboat. Such punishments horrified the Indians, who, although quick to torture, mutilate, and murder their enemies, did not as a rule punish children or others who broke rules within their own community.

Today nineteenth-century punishments seem extreme. For mutiny or desertion, a guilty party could be shot or hanged by the thumbs. Individuals could be chained in dark solitary-confinement cells for very small offenses. Prisons in Europe and America were filthy, overcrowded, and unsupervised; even a short jail sentence could be every bit as cruel as a round of lashes.

CHAPTER 4
THE GREAT ADVENTURE

In the fall of 1803, William Clark established winter camp on the east bank of the Mississippi River at Camp Dubois (Camp Wood) in Illinois. There he spent months organizing and drilling the men. For their expedition to succeed, the men needed to learn to work together and follow the orders of their officers.

Finally, the Corps dipped its paddles in the water of the Mississippi River at 4 p.m. on May 14, 1804. With Clark in charge of the 55-foot (16.8-meter) keelboat and with a pirogue on either side, they headed west and rowed up the muddy Missouri River. Lewis hiked cross-country from St. Louis to meet the rest of the Corps. He had been in St. Louis on March 9 and 10, serving as chief witness to the official transfer of the Louisiana Territories from France to the United States.

At last, they were on their way. The work of pushing the heavy keelboat and the pirogues against the current of the wild river was extraordinarily difficult, but being on their way at last was exhilarating.

The expedition—or at least one of its leaders—nearly had an untimely end just as it was getting started. On May 23, just two days after pausing at St. Charles, the last French settlement on the Missouri, Lewis was exploring overland while Clark and the men struggled up the river in the boats. Lewis attempted to scale a 300-foot (91-meter) bluff but lost his footing. He started to fall, a plunge that would probably have killed him. Fortunately, he was able to catch himself by pulling out his knife and plunging it into the cliff face.

On May 25, the Corps passed the last white settlement on the Missouri. Soon it paddled by the home of pathfinder

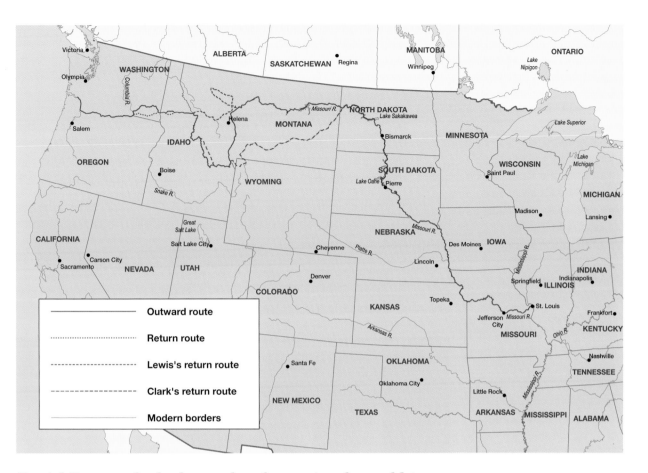

Daniel Boone, who had moved as far west as he could to avoid neighbors.

The great river challenged the men. Uprooted trees floated down its middle; hidden sandbars upset the keelboat; the riverbank sometimes collapsed unexpectedly. Storms thundered across the prairie, and the river rose in height and increased in speed, flooding the countryside.

On June 4, Sergeant John Ordway, who otherwise proved steady and reliable, steered the keelboat too close to shore. Its mast snapped in an overhanging "Secamore tree." With typical Corps humor, they christened a nearby stream "Mast Creek" in honor of Ordway's piloting. After making repairs, the Corps continued the journey up the Missouri.

By mid-July, the explorers had reached present-day Nebraska, still without sighting Indians. By then they had established routines for their work and made progress. Minor problems occurred: Men were sick with colds, blisters, and "tumers." Private Alexander Willard was

Lewis and Clark's epic trek from St. Louis, Missouri to the Pacific coast and back lasted from 1804 until 1806.

25

In December 1803, Captain William Clark and his Corps recruits built a camp along the Mississippi at the mouth of the Dubois River. The location was strategically important: It was close to the mouth of the Missouri River, which the Corps planned to follow. It was east of the Mississippi, so it was not on Louisiana Purchase territory. This was important. Clark wanted to follow rules set by the commandant overseeing Louisiana that stated that the Corps would not enter the territory until it was transferred to the U.S. government. Camp Dubois was a military installation, and the men spent their months there training and performing military duties. A replica of the camp has been constructed at the Lewis and Clark State Historic Site near Hartford, Illinois (map reference 13). The park also includes a visitor's center with exhibits devoted to the Corps of Discovery, including a full-size replica of the keelboat used on the expedition.

discovered sleeping on guard and sentenced to one hundred lashes (twenty-five lashes per night for four nights). Clark lost several days' notes during a storm, and he was "much put to it to Recolect the Courses."

As they traveled, the men found plants, mammals, and birds that were new to them. Having no other means to capture and study them, they killed a badger and a coyote and stuffed the hides before they shipped them to Jefferson in the spring. They shot a white pelican and were amazed that the pouch beneath its bill held 5 gallons (18.9 liters) of water.

Fighting mosquito swarms and a relentless, blistering sun, the men gradually made their way upriver. On August 2, the Corps at last encountered inhabitants of

Above: **The full-scale replica of the keelboat *Discovery* on Blue Lake at the Lewis and Clark State Park (map reference 15).**

"these empty lands." The first Native Americans to meet Lewis and Clark's party were members of the Missouri and Oto bands. These tribes had been almost wiped out by smallpox, a disease that they had probably caught from white trappers and traders. They numbered only about 250 people. These farmers and buffalo hunters lived in oven-shaped, earth-covered houses grouped in towns. They appeared at the Corps's camp near what is now Council Bluffs, Iowa.

Lewis invited six or seven of the chiefs to a council the next morning. In preparation, the Corps put up flags and used the main sail of the keelboat for an awning. When the chiefs were seated and contentedly smoking, the soldiers marched in. They wore their best uniforms, and they demonstrated their shooting skills. Then Lewis made a speech, with Corps member George Drouillard interpreting in sign language. He said that the Indian nations were "children" of a new "great father" in Washington who would provide trade goods and protection

Opposite: **The Lewis and Clark State Memorial in Alton, Illinois, (formerly Camp Wood) commemorates the start of the expedition.**

Historical reenactors row a keelboat down the Missouri River during Lewis and Clark Heritage Days in St. Charles, Missouri (map reference 9). This picture gives a good indication of the size of these rugged craft.

in place of their formerly unreliable commerce with the French and Spanish. By journey's end, Lewis had given this speech many times.

Lewis told the Indians a great river of trade would flow if the Missouri and Oto made peace with their neighbors. He urged the chiefs to visit President Jefferson. Then, each chief received gifts, including a peace medal and face paint.

Indian encounters did not always go so smoothly. On August 18, the principal chiefs of the Missouri and Oto, Big Horse and Little Thief, listened to Lewis's speech. Big Horse then asked for larger gifts and for whiskey. Lewis responded with the usual tobacco, face paint, and beads, and the warriors left unhappy. Nevertheless, Little Thief indicated he would go to Washington. (In March 1805, a delegation including Little Thief met with Jefferson. He, too, promised them trade goods and told them of his hope for peace among the nations.)

By mid-August, Sergeant Charles Floyd was suffering. Pain in his abdomen became so severe that for days he lay in the bottom of a canoe and ate nothing. With their limited knowledge of medicine, the captains could not help him, and on August 20, he died. (It is now thought that he succumbed to an infection caused by a ruptured appendix.) He was the only Corps member to die on the journey.

SERGEANT FLOYD MONUMENT

Amazingly, only one Corps of Discovery member—Sergeant Charles Floyd—died during the journey, and he was the victim of a ruptured appendix. Though he was part of the expedition for only a short time, he has been celebrated with the largest gravesite monument—larger even than that for William Clark, who enjoyed a successful career in government after the journey west. The Sergeant Floyd Monument, a 100-foot (30.5-meter) stone obelisk, sits on a bluff top in Sioux City, Iowa (map reference 10); the site offers a spectacular view of the Missouri River. The nearby Lewis and Clark Interpretive Center is a new museum that tells the story of the Corps of Discovery.

The Sergeant Floyd Memorial marks the grave of Sergeant Charles Floyd, Jr.

During this part of the journey, except for a fringe of trees along the river, the prairie opened up wide on both sides of the Missouri. The men saw herds of buffalo, elk, and pronghorn antelope. Because they were working very hard, their appetites were enormous, and the captains sent hunters out in search of game every day. The men ate as much as nine pounds (four kilograms) of meat per day—each!

Toiling upriver, the explorers encountered endless miles of prickly pear cactus that made hunting or walking an ordeal. At night, wolf packs howled. During the day, the Corps discovered magpies and prairie dogs. Clark measured the skeleton of a "fish" that was 45 feet (13.7 meters) long—actually the fossilized remains of a pleisosaur, an ocean-dwelling dinosaur. For two weeks, the youngest member of the Corps, eighteen-year-old George Shannon, was lost.

Fall evenings were cold on the prairie, and Clark issued a flannel shirt to each man. The cold was not their

A Sioux encampment. This late eighteenth-century image shows the way a group of tepees looks. The proud man in front of his lodge is an Oglala Sioux, Tashun-Kakokipa, which translates as "Young Man Afraid of his Horses."

principal concern, however. Soon they expected to meet the Sioux, and the Sioux made them nervous. Unlike the Missouri and the Oto, who had been decimated by disease, the Sioux were numerous and warlike. The men worried that they might not settle for ribbons and beads.

In the middle of what is today South Dakota, the Corps met the Teton Sioux. The Sioux served a meal of dog (which they considered a delicacy), gave ritual speeches, and then smoked pipes with the captains. Lewis and Clark presented medals to the tribal leaders, but the Sioux were not satisfied with trinkets. They knew the captains had modern weapons and liquor. There was a heated exchange, and the Sioux attempted to hold the keelboat and pirogues. The Corps squared off against several hundred warriors.

John Ordway later wrote, "Some had fire arms. Some had Spears. Some had a kind of cutlashes [sword], and all the rest had Bows and steel or Iron pointed arrows." Captain Lewis drew his sword and briefly considered cutting the ropes holding the boats and giving his men the order to fire. Captain Clark found himself surrounded by armed Sioux but remained calm.

Finally, the tension between the two sides eased, and the captains gave the Sioux extra tobacco from their already dwindling supply. With warriors watching, the nervous Corps paddled upstream. Had the confrontation not ended well, they realized, the expedition could have failed at this very early date.

Soon the Corps entered the lands of the Arikara and Mandan, tribes of farmers and hunters who lived in settled towns. The captains gave more speeches, fired the air gun, and flew the American flag. The men paraded and

Pencil sketch of a Mandan Indian earthlodge by Karl Bodmer

distributed gifts. In the mornings, there was frost; winter was approaching.

At this point in the journey, York, William Clark's slave, started to appear in Corps journal entries. The tribes the Corps encountered had never seen a black man, and they were impressed. "Those Indians wer much astonished at my Servent," Clark wrote. "They never Saw a black man before, all flocked around him & examind him from top to toe, he Carried on the joke and made himself more turribal than we wished him to doe."

Enjoying his temporary freedom and equality, York became an ambassador to the Native Americans, who were delighted with him. Among them, he could relax and have fun (all of which apparently irritated his owner).

When snow fell on October 23, Lewis and Clark realized they must make a winter camp. The river would soon freeze, and travel would be impossible. They entered into negotiations with the Mandan and Arikara near what today is Washburn, North Dakota. Amid steadily falling temperatures, they pulled their boats out of the water and built Fort Mandan across the river from the principal Indian town.

CHAPTER 5
FORT MANDAN

The winter of 1804–1805 was bitter on the northern reaches of the Missouri River. Blown by a remorseless wind, snow and sleet fell without letup. Temperatures plunged below zero, and frostbite was a real risk to fingers and toes.

Fort Mandan was not large or especially warm, but its palisade and rough barracks provided shelter from the howling storms. Inside its walls, the captains brought their journals and observations up to date, while the men hunted buffalo and traded with the Arikara and Mandan for corn and beans. The men were often cold and sometimes hungry, but the Indians were friendly, and the Corps spent enjoyable evenings singing, dancing, and romancing young women from the tribe.

In December the temperature fell to 45 degrees below zero (minus 25 degrees Celsius). To the suffering white men, the Native Americans seemed impervious to the weather. "Customs & the habits of those people has anured [them] to bare more Cold than I thought it possible for man to endure," Clark noted.

During the cold winter at Fort Mandan, Lewis and Clark made plans for their journey to start again in the spring. Because Moses Reed and John Newman had been dismissed and would be sent home, the Corps would be short two men. The Corps was also entering territory in which they would encounter Native Americans whose languages were unfamiliar. To solve both problems, the captains hired resident French-Canadian trappers Jean Baptiste LePage and Toussaint Charbonneau as interpreters. LePage enlisted in the army as a private but was eventually judged by Lewis to be a man of "no

Inside one of the
reconstructed huts
at Fort Mandan
(map reference 20)

particular merit." The captains thought even less of Charbonneau, who, like the Corps's designated hunter and scout George Drouillard, remained a nonmilitary member.

Charbonneau was forty-seven and the oldest member of the expedition. He was not particularly energetic or courageous, and the captains barely tolerated him. It was fortunate that he was retained, because his eighteen-year-old Shoshone wife, Sacagawea, soon proved valuable to the Corps. Charbonneau had purchased Sacagawea (loosely translated as "Bird Woman") from the Hidatsa, who had bought the girl after she had been captured in a Sioux raid on the Shoshone. In the winter of 1805, inside the captains' hut at Fort Mandan, Sacagawea gave birth to a boy.

Captain Clark and his men
building a line of huts.
From *Journal of Voyages*

Above: **Reconstructed cabin at Fort Mandan**

Below: **Lewis Meriwether wearing clothes made from animal pelts**

Charbonneau named him Jean Baptiste, but Clark called him "Pompey" for his "little dancing boy antics." Pompey was fifty-five days old when he departed with the Corps for the Pacific.

An event in March 1805 set the tone for Charbonneau's relationship with Lewis and Clark. Charbonneau informed the captains that he would no longer stand guard duty and that he would not carry a pack on the journey ahead. Furthermore, he said that if he had any difficulty with any Corps member, he would immediately leave the expedition. The captains replied that his requests were unreasonable, and Charbonneau, along with his wife and child, was escorted out of the fort. Within a few days, however, the Frenchman said he was sorry, that he would do all things as directed, and that he wished to return. The captains relented, and the Charbonneau family moved back inside Fort Mandan.

On April 7, Corporal Richard Warfington took a dozen men in the keelboat and began the return trip to St. Louis. He carried the Corps's collections for President Jefferson: various plants, stuffed animals, and miscellaneous items they had found or had been given (buffalo robes, samples of Mandan corn, pronghorn and bear skins, insects, mice, live magpies, a prairie chicken, and antlers of elk and bighorn sheep).

FORT MANDAN

William Clark's journal entry for November 3, 1804, is a simple note: "We commence building our cabins." On this day, the Corps started constructing the fort that would be their home for several months, over a long and bitterly cold winter. Fort Mandan (map reference 20) was an important stop on the journey for many reasons. Because it was built in the midst of the Mandan-Hidatsa villages, it gave the whites their first look inside Native American culture. The fort was also the place where they hired trapper Toussaint Charbonneau and his wife, Sacagawea; in fact, she gave birth to her son, Jean Baptiste, in the fort. Today, a full-sized replica of the fort has been reconstructed on its original site near Washburn, North Dakota. The nearby interpretive center offers an in-depth look at the Lewis and Clark expedition and the lives of the northern Plains Indian tribes.

"We Proceed On . . ."

The phrase "we proceed on" is found often in the journals of the expedition. On April 8, 1805, the Corps of Discovery —now with a woman and a child—pushed away from shore and into the unknown.

In six canoes and two pirogues, the men paddled toward the setting sun, fighting mosquitoes and biting gnats, sandstorms, and a baking sun. The landscape presented puzzling choices of routes, and the riverbanks became steeper and more difficult as the explorers made their way through the Missouri Breaks and toward the Great Falls.

The men were curious about a large bear that the Native Americans feared and hunted with extreme caution. They had seen several at a distance and were eager to kill and examine one. The Corps believed that Indian accounts of the bears were exaggerated, perhaps because they considered themselves superior to the Indians (who, in their journals, they refer to as "savages"). They were also accustomed to the smaller and shyer black bear found east of the Mississippi River. They called these large animals "white bears," but we know them today as grizzly bears. Their first encounter with a grizzly was frightening and nearly resulted in the death of several Corps members, including Lewis. Afterward they were more respectful. The bear was, Lewis wrote, a "furious and formidable animal."

UPPER MISSOURI BREAKS NATIONAL MONUMENT

The remote section of the Missouri River in eastern Montana (map reference 25), noted for its beautiful white cliffs, might be the only part of Lewis and Clark's route that remains largely unchanged since the expedition passed through two centuries ago. The river flows for 149 miles (240 kilometers) through a region rich with scenery, wildlife, and history. The best way to experience it is in a canoe. Paddling here offers one of the few opportunities to recreate what the Corps saw and experienced on its journey to the Pacific. A variety of outfitters provide guided overnight trips, canoe rentals, and shuttle service on the river.

Sacagawea, from a drawing by E. S. Paxson

The men found themselves traveling through a land of plenty. They ate buffalo (sometimes consuming only its tongue), elk, deer, and pronghorn. Beaver tail was an occasional delicacy. They tried exotic fare as well, raiding the nests of geese and even bald eagles for eggs.

In mid-June, the canoes halted at the Great Falls of the Missouri, a multistepped waterfall that towered 80 feet (24 meters) above the lower river and could not be traveled by boat alone. For the next month, therefore, the men unloaded the canoes, hauled their gear and the canoes themselves around these extensive waterfalls, and reloaded the boats when they had been carried past the obstacles to open water, a process known as a portage. They set off up the river again—only to discover more falls and the need to portage once again around the barrier. Hauling boats and cargo around on land was exhausting labor. Their moccasins wore out, their clothes shredded, blisters covered their hands and feet, and rattlesnakes were everywhere.

Shortly after portaging around the falls, the men were assaulted by a slashing thunder and hail storm that left them bleeding and bruised. Clark was away exploring with Charbonneau and Sacagawea (who was carrying her baby) when the storm struck. They took shelter in a ravine, but within minutes, the heavy rain started a flash flood. The three explorers climbed frantically up the sides of the ravine to escape the fast-rising water. They lost most of their possessions: Clark, his invaluable compass;

Sacagawea, her baby's soft bearskin swaddling; and Charbonneau, his gun and his nerve, for he was "much Scared and narely without motion," wrote John Ordway.

With the storm behind them, the Corps continued their journey upstream. The river was becoming shallow, and there were signs of mountains ahead. The Missouri began to run faster and cleaner, like a mountain stream, without the load of silt that characterizes the "Big Muddy," as it is known in its lower reaches. The river took them past cliffs and into deep canyons. In early August, endless rows of

After Pehriska-Ruhpa, Moennitarri Warrior in the Costume of the Dog Danse **by Karl Bodmer. This is one of four paintings from the 1930s by the Swiss-born artist in the Sioux City Lewis and Clark Interpretive Center of Plains Indians (map reference 10).**

snow-capped peaks could be seen rising in the distance.

The men were sick from unknown fevers, blistered, bitten, and exhausted. The sight of high, cool mountains renewed their spirits, and Sacagawea began to recognize landmarks, for she was nearing her homeland. The men realized that soon they would need horses to climb over the mountains before winter trapped them in some high-altitude pass.

The need for horses meant trading with the Shoshone tribe, whose language they had not yet encountered. Lewis and Clark knew they had to overcome a large communication barrier but hoped that several people added during the journey would help solve the problem. Communicating with the Shoshone ended up being a complicated process, but it worked. Sacagawea spoke to the Shoshone and then translated their response into Hidatsa for Charbonneau; he translated the words into French. Finally, Private Francois Labiche made the final translation for the captains, who spoke only English.

At the foot of the Rockies, the expedition encountered the Shoshone and their chief, Cameahwait. Because the Corps traveled with a woman and a baby, the Indians recognized that the group was not a war party and met them on peaceful terms. What followed was one of the most remarkable incidents in the history of the Corps of Discovery. As the parties gathered to bargain for horses, Sacagawea recognized Cameahwait—she realized that he was her brother, even though she had not seen him for years and had been carried hundreds of miles from her original home when she had been captured by the Sioux and sold to the Hidatsa! During the emotional homecoming, the chief agreed to provide horses and a guide to lead the Corps over the rugged Bitterroot Mountains along what has become the modern-day border between Montana and Idaho. After a brief rest, the Corps—including Sacagawea and Pompey—followed their guide into the trackless mountains.

THE GREAT FALLS OF THE MISSOURI

Among the many challenges faced by the Corps of Discovery, the month-long portage around the roaring Great Falls of the Missouri River was one of the most difficult. There were five waterfalls plus rapids. All the canoes had to be unloaded and the boats and gear carried for several miles on foot over difficult terrain around the barrier. The Corps frequently encountered rattlesnakes and grizzly bears. The job took a month to complete and nearly robbed the men of the morale they needed to finish their journey. Visitors can still see the falls and retrace the steps of the portaging Corps. The U.S. Forest Service's Lewis and Clark Interpretive Center offers a glimpse of the world as it looked while the Corps was passing through in 1805.

Opposite: A diorama at the Lewis and Clark National Historic Trail Interpretive Center (map reference 12) of men hauling a dugout canoe up a steep embankment

Left: Plaque at Camp Fortunate Overlook above Clark Canyon Reservoir, where Lewis and Clark and the Corps of Discovery met with Shoshone Indians

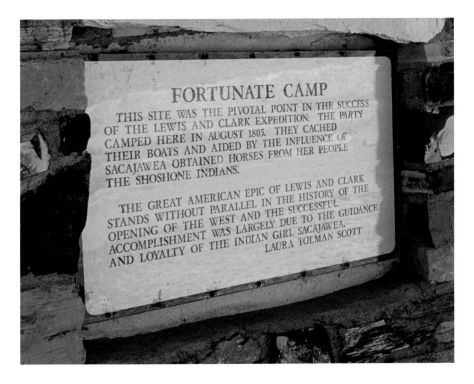

FORTUNATE CAMP

THIS SITE WAS THE PIVOTAL POINT IN THE SUCCESS OF THE LEWIS AND CLARK EXPEDITION. THE PARTY CAMPED HERE IN AUGUST 1805. THEY CACHED THEIR BOATS AND AIDED BY THE INFLUENCE OF SACAJAWEA OBTAINED HORSES FROM HER PEOPLE THE SHOSHONE INDIANS.

THE GREAT AMERICAN EPIC OF LEWIS AND CLARK STANDS WITHOUT PARALLEL IN THE HISTORY OF THE OPENING OF THE WEST AND THE SUCCESSFUL ACCOMPLISHMENT WAS LARGELY DUE TO THE GUIDANCE AND LOYALTY OF THE INDIAN GIRL SACAJAWEA.
LAURA TOLMAN SCOTT

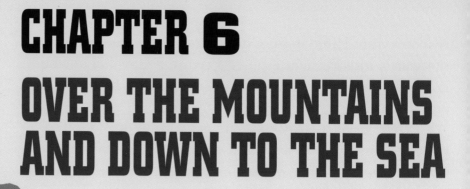

CHAPTER 6
OVER THE MOUNTAINS AND DOWN TO THE SEA

The nature of the journey changed immediately as the Corps climbed into the mountains. On the Great Plains, the explorers had suffered from intense heat and annoying insects, but game was abundant. In the mountains, they experienced numbing cold and snow, the insects disappeared, and game seemed to be nonexistent. They would struggle to travel all day, then collapse after dark in a wet, hungry, and fireless camp. Within a few days, they considered eating their horses.

The Bitterroot Mountains were a challenge like no other the Corps had faced. They were steep, rocky, and barren of food. The men fought through the rugged countryside, tearing their moccasins and their clothes. Horses and men fell; packs crashed down cliffs. The mountains are "fatiguing almost beyond description," Patrick Gass wrote.

"Some places so steep and rockey," said John Ordway, "that some of the horses fell backwards and roled to the bottom. one horse was near being killed....eat the last of our pork &.C. some of the men threaten to kill a colt to eat they being hungry, but puts it off untill tomorrow noon hopeing the hunters will kill Some game....so we lay down wet hungry and cold came with much fatigue."

By late September, the explorers were so hungry that they shot and ate a horse. They also ate sparrows, fish, the last of their portable soup, and one unlucky wolf. They even gnawed on candles. They were soon completely out of food, and the Shoshone guide provided by Cameahwait deserted them. Things looked bleak. Then, however, they met the Nez Perce tribe led by Chief Twisted Hair, and their fortunes changed.

Beacon Rock towers above the Columbia River, where Lewis and Clark first witnessed tide effects on their exploration of the Pacific Northwest.

The Nez Perce could have killed them and seized their weapons and horses. According to legend, the Indians considered this option. Instead, they decided to share what they had with the ragged and desperate explorers and then lead them to the safety of their village. The Nez Perce also showed the Corps a native root, the camas, that could be used for food. When dried, ground, and baked, camas produced a type of bread. Lewis and Clark's men gobbled the camas bread . . . and immediately became ill. They quickly recovered from their upset stomachs, and the kindness of the Nez Perce helped them make it through the mountains.

West of the Continental Divide, the journey was much easier. Rivers flowed toward the Pacific Ocean, and the men could float easily and quickly toward their destination. The Indians were also very friendly. Twisted Hair agreed to keep the Corps's horses safe until they returned in the spring. Chief Yellepit of the Walla Walla nation helped them build canoes and threw a party that was attended by members of the neighboring Yakima tribe. There the Corps and the Native Americans feasted on salmon and dog. Yellepit presented Clark with a white horse; in return, Clark gave the man his sword.

As the Corps approached the Pacific, they began to move much more quickly, but there was still considerable danger. Native Americans crowded the banks of the rocky and

THE BITTERROOTS AND THE LOST TRAIL

One of the most challenging parts of the westward journey—and still one of the most mysterious—was the Corps's struggle through the Bitterroot Mountains (map reference 1). They traversed some very rugged territory in what is now southwestern Montana. This area is now a mixture of private property and national forests and can be explored by car or on foot. A walk on one of the area's spectacular trails will give the modern-day hiker a sense of just what the Corps faced as they fought their way through these mountains in September 1805 with no trail to follow.

Sacajawea Guiding the Lewis and Clark Expedition by Alfred Russell. Sacagawea's name has been spelled many different ways. The editor of the Lewis and Clark journals spelled it with a "j" instead of a "g," and that spelling was used for many years. Recently, historians have preferred Sacagawea because it means "bird woman" (her nickname) in Hidasta. Some paintings and parks in her honor still use the old spelling.

treacherous Snake River to watch the foolhardy white men test the river's whitewater. The Indians were sure the explorers would drown among the river's many boulders. The men of the Corps pushed onward toward their destination, which they believed was near. Despite overturned canoes and a close brush with death in the

A map of some of the area covered by the expedition west of the Mississippi River. The Lewis River, now the Snake River between Idaho and Oregon, and the Columbia River are depicted. The map was drawn by expedition member Robert Frazer in 1811.

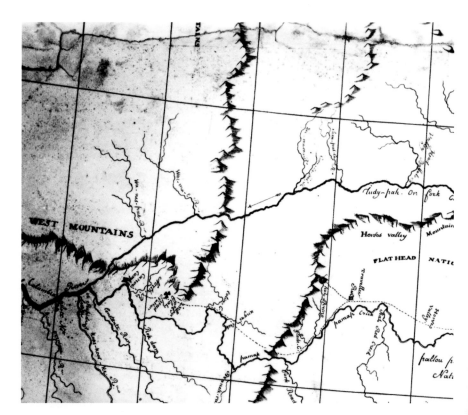

SACAJAWEA STATE PARK

On October 16, 1805, the Corps finally reached the mighty Columbia River, their final avenue to the Pacific Ocean. The explorers camped for two days at the confluence of the Snake and Columbia Rivers. They repaired equipment, hunted for food, and spent time with a local Native American tribe. Then they started the final push to their destination. The area where they camped is now a Washington state park named in honor of the Shoshone teenager who was the only female member of the Corps (map reference 23). The park includes an interpretive center and a long stretch of scenic shoreline along both rivers.

Above: **An expedition marker in Sacajawea State Park, Washington**

roaring rapids, the captains kept on course. On October 16, they entered the broad Columbia River.

Every member of Lewis and Clark's team was excited. They sped through the homelands of the Wishram and Wasco Indians. In the evenings, the Natives marveled at the black man, York, and were astonished by the great dog, Seaman. They screamed merrily when Pierre Cruzatte played the fiddle and danced. John Collins, who had once received one hundred lashes for tapping the Corps's whiskey barrel while on guard, made beer from a local root. On October 20, John Ordway recorded that the Corps paddled an astonishing 46 miles (74 kilometers)!

Soon they passed two well-known (then) dormant volcanoes: Mount Hood, on their left, and Mount St. Helens, on their right. Clark incorrectly noted in his journal that Mount St. Helens was "perhaps the highest pinical in America." (It was actually much lower than

Mount Hood and not even as tall as the highest peak in the Bitterroots.) On November 3, they detected the rise and fall of the tide in the river. A few days later, Clark wrote: "We are all wet and disagreeable, had large fires made on the Stone and dried our bedding and kill the flees, which collected in our blankets at every old village we encamped near." The men's excitement at finishing the journey could hardly be contained; they strained forward toward the ocean.

As they drew near the Pacific, however, heavy fog, clouds of biting flies, and continual rain dampened the Corps's spirits. They were wet day and night in the gray mist, and they occasionally lost their way. On seeing the great ocean at last, the object of all their efforts, the men named the spot "Cape Disappointment." Although they were wet, cold, hungry, and bewildered by the gray murk, the captains nevertheless held a vote to decide their next steps.

The vote was held to aid the Corps's search for an appropriate place to spend the upcoming winter. The

A painting of Lewis and Clark at the mouth of the Columbia River during their exploration of the Louisiana Territory by Frederic Remington

group had explored both the north and south banks of the Columbia but could not agree on what to do next. To the east, snow and ice blocked the mountain passes, so returning before spring was out of the question. Although they knew commercial traders visited the mouth of the Columbia River, no ships were in sight. On November 24, the captains asked everyone in the expedition to vote on where they should set up winter quarters. Even Sacagawea and York were invited to take part. The majority voted for the south side of the Columbia for a variety of reasons. They would best be able to make salt, which was needed for seasoning and preserving food, at that location. The south shore also offered the best place from which to observe any sailing ship that might visit the Columbia. Finally, elk, deer, and other food sources were more plentiful there.

The vote marked the first time a woman cast a ballot in a free election in America. It was also the first recorded vote for people of color.

CAPE DISAPPOINTMENT

After their epic journey across most of the continent, the Corps was initially elated when, on November 7, 1805, they first spied the object of their efforts, the Pacific Ocean. Their high spirits were soon dashed by bad weather, annoying insects, and a rugged, largely inaccessible coastline. The men gave the spit of land at the junction of the Columbia River's north bank and the ocean a name that suited their mood: Cape Disappointment. They soon abandoned the cape in favor of the south bank of the river as the place to build their winter quarters. Today, Cape Disappointment (map reference 2) is a spectacularly scenic Washington state park, complete with an interpretive center dedicated to the Lewis and Clark journey.

Sacagawea interprets Lewis and Clark's intentions to the Chinook Indians.

CHAPTER 7
WINTER QUARTERS AND JOURNEY HOME

No ship appeared, so the Corps built a 50-foot by 50-foot (15-meter) square enclosure they called Fort Clatsop after the friendly Indians of the neighborhood. (When they departed in the spring of 1806, the captains left the fort and its furniture to a Clatsop chief named Coboway.) All winter, they huddled around their fires, struggling to feed themselves, to dry their clothes, and to occupy their time. They suffered through fleas, miserable weather, and constant sickness.

Relations were less cordial with the Chinook, the Native group living north of the Columbia. Accustomed to white traders who visited the Pacific coast in ships, the Chinook charged high prices for dried fish and venison. They also stole from the Corps, which angered the explorers. The decision to build the fort on the south side of the river away from the Chinook turned out to be in everyone's best interest.

The Corps passed its winter on the Pacific in damp, cramped quarters without enough to eat. The wretched conditions contributed to negative attitudes among the men. As early as December 1, Clark wrote: "My hunters returned without any thing saw 2 gang of Elk a disagreeable situation, men all employed in mending their leather clothes, socks &c....The sea which is imedeately in front roars like a repeeted roling thunder and have rored in that way ever since our arrival...I cant say Pasific as since I have seen it, it has been the reverse."

By March 1806, no trading vessel had appeared, and conditions at the fort were little short of appalling. Although snow was still falling in the mountains, it was time to start for home. Having used up the trade goods that Lewis so carefully assembled to buy food, the Corps

FORT CLATSOP

The Corps's third and final winter encampment was clearly the most dismal. The weather was damp and gloomy. Food and other supplies were desperately lacking, and, having reached their destination, most of the men just wanted to go home. The Corps abandoned Fort Clatsop in late March and started paddling eastward up the Columbia. The departure probably lifted the men's spirits, but they left far too early. The explorers would soon find their progress stalled for weeks waiting for deep mountain snows to melt. In the 1950s, Oregon residents rebuilt a replica of Fort Clatsop (map reference 14), following dimensions and descriptions from William Clark's journal. The fort—along with an interesting exhibit showing how the men made salt by boiling seawater—is part of the new Lewis and Clark National Historical Park.

The reconstructed fort at Fort Clatsop National Memorial

had almost nothing to barter. Lewis exchanged the jacket of his uniform and some tobacco for a Clatsop canoe. Sacagawea traded her blue, beaded belt. Even their friends, the Clatsop people, wanted more than the Corps could afford for a second canoe. The captains sent a party to steal one from the Natives. They justified their theft as payment for six elk that the Clatsop had stolen from the fort earlier in the winter. On March 22, the Corps posted a list of its members inside Fort Clatsop as a record of the expedition for anybody who might someday find the empty

The confluence of the Missouri and Marias Rivers viewed from Decision Point, where explorer William Clark stood during the expedition

building. The men stowed their meager belongings in the canoes and pushed off upstream.

Retracing their steps, the Corps again encountered the Wishram and the Walla Walla tribes, and once again they arrived hungry. In exchange for food, Clark doctored the sick. Because the Indians viewed York as a powerful sorcerer and warrior, he was sent to bargain for scraps of dog meat and roots.

The captains led the men steadily toward the mountains. Within two months, they were again among the Nez Perce, the people who had kept their horses and the gear they did not need for their paddle downstream. The men were impatient to hike over the mountains, but blizzards still swept through the higher elevations. So they waited, reduced to begging for food.

On May 26, Patrick Gass wrote, "Our stock of provisions is exhausted, and we have nothing to eat but some roots, which we get from the natives at a very dear rate." They cut the brass buttons off their clothing in exchange for these roots and dog meat.

Lewis and Clark used a saltwork like this to boil seawater down to salt.

For a month, they waited. Then, in early June, the captains could no longer restrain the men's eagerness . . . or their own. Despite warnings from the Nez Perce that the trail would not be open for another month, the Corps climbed again into the Bitterroot Mountains. Immediately, they encountered deep snow. Soon the snow reached 14 feet (4.3 meters) deep, and the men found themselves in a storm of sleet and hail. Numb and shivering, they turned back.

Two weeks later, they trudged upward again into the rapidly melting snow. By the first of July, they reached their old camp at "Traveler's Rest." Spirits soared, for now they were truly on their way home.

Still high in the mountains, the captains took a risk. To study a greater part of these new U.S. lands, they divided the Corps. Lewis took a small crew and headed north to look for a shortcut to the upper Missouri by way of the Marias River. It is possible that he was still hoping to find the fabled Northwest Passage. Staying with the majority of the Corps, Clark hiked due east, planning to follow the Yellowstone River to the Missouri. They agreed to rendezvous later on the Missouri.

On July 8, 1806, Clark's group reached a cache of canoes and provisions the Corps had left on the Beaverhead River. Everything was damp but safe. Clark now further split his party into two groups. He put Sergeant Ordway in charge of a body of ten men paddling six canoes loaded with supplies. They floated back down the Missouri River with instructions for meeting Lewis's party and for finding Clark again. Clark took the remaining Corps members and started overland

This statue is located in Fort Benton, Montana, facing the Missouri River. It is Montana's official state memorial to Lewis, Clark, and Sacagawea.

A Blackfoot chief and his wife haul a litter on which a young woman rides

toward the Yellowstone River. Once on the Yellowstone, he planned to build canoes and float downstream to that river's meeting with the Missouri.

In traveling to the Yellowstone, Clark was not sure which direction to go. Sacagawea, whose homeland they were again passing through, pointed south, through what is now Bozeman Pass in Montana. Clark took Sacagawea's advice. It was a fortunate decision because other possible routes would have proven much more difficult.

On the Yellowstone, Clark's men built dugout canoes and marveled at the immense herds of buffalo. They estimated seeing ten thousand animals in one herd. It was here on the plains of the Yellowstone that Clark inscribed his name and the date on a sandstone formation beside the river. He called the landmark "Pompy's Tower" in honor of Sacagawea's son. Although the men had carved their names on trees along the route, Clark's inscription remains the only surviving physical evidence the Corps of Discovery left on the landscape.

POMPEYS PILLAR NATIONAL MONUMENT

An eye-catching sandstone butte east of Billings, Montana, features the only known surviving physical evidence of the passage of the Corps of Discovery. On July 25, 1806, while traveling down the Yellowstone River on the return leg of the journey, Captain William Clark paused at the rock long enough to carve his name and the date. He called the butte "Pompy's Tower"; Nicholas Biddle, first editor of the Lewis and Clark journals, changed the name to Pompeys Pillar. Pioneer James Stuart discovered Clark's signature in 1863; the site was set aside as a national monument in 2001. A nearby attraction is the Little Bighorn Battlefield (map reference 16), site of George Armstrong Custer's defeat at the hands of the Sioux in 1876. Three years earlier, Custer and his troops had been camped by Pompeys Pillar (map reference 21) and were enjoying a refreshing swim in the Yellowstone when they were fired on by Sioux Indians.

Pompeys Pillar National Monument

Meanwhile, Lewis traveled north along the Blackfoot River and recrossed the Continental Divide at what is now Lewis and Clark Pass. Amid cold and stormy weather, he reached the Marias River, more than 300 miles (483 kilometers) distant from the main party.

Walking toward the Missouri in late July, Lewis spotted eight Blackfeet warriors. Although he had hoped to miss these people (whose reputation as warriors was formidable), he could not avoid a meeting. That night, the white and Indian parties shared a campfire, but all were

Mih-Tutta-Hangkusch, a Mandan Village, a painting by Karl Bodmer

wary. The next morning the explorers woke just as the Blackfeet were stealing their horses and guns. In the fight that followed, two Blackfeet were killed. This was the only act of bloodshed during the expedition.

Lewis left a Jefferson peace medal around the neck of one of the corpses "that they might be informed who we were." Then for twenty-four hours, he and his three men rode hard toward the Missouri and their rendezvous with the rest of the Corps. Luckily, they encountered no more Blackfeet.

On the plains, game was again plentiful. On August 11, Lewis spotted elk in the thickets by the river. He took Pierre Cruzatte to help replenish their meat supply. As Lewis aimed, the nearsighted Cruzatte fired—somehow the private mistook Lewis for an elk—and the shot struck the captain. Amazingly, the ball passed through Lewis's buttocks without cutting an artery or shattering a bone. The wound was painful, perhaps embarrassing, but it was not fatal.

The next day, just downstream from the Yellowstone and with Lewis lying awkwardly on his chest in the canoe to protect his wound, the Corps reunited and began its dash for home.

They halted at the villages of the Mandan where they had wintered more than a year before. There, Charbonneau, Sacagawea, and Pompey departed. The captains also released John Colter. Colter returned to the Yellowstone River to trap beaver, to discover a magnificent land that would someday become Yellowstone National Park, and to establish the tradition of the "mountain man" in U.S. folklore.

Clark and Lewis were supposed to recruit Indian chiefs to travel to Washington and meet their new "great father," Thomas Jefferson. The tribes were at war, however, and even though a few accepted the invitation, this was a difficult challenge.

Into September, the Corps sped down the Missouri. The men were eager to reach St. Louis; some days they paddled 70 miles (113 kilometers). Now they met many traders

JEAN BAPTISTE "POMPEY" CHARBONNEAU

Jean Baptiste Charbonneau was born in the hut occupied by Lewis and Clark at Fort Mandan on February 11, 1805. His parents were the French-Canadian fur trapper Toussaint Charbonneau and the Shoshone woman Sacagawea. He survived the trip to the Pacific and back to the Mandan villages, winning William Clark's enduring affection for his antics. Clark nicknamed him "Pompey" or "Pomp."

When Charbonneau and Sacagawea left the Corps on August 17, 1806, Clark offered to raise Jean Baptiste as his own son. The child was not yet weaned, however, and Sacagawea promised to bring him to Clark at a later date.

In a letter to Charbonneau, Clark wrote: "As to your little Son (my boy Pomp) you well know my fondness for him and my anxiety to take and raise him as my own child. I once more tell you if you will bring your son Baptiest to me I will educate him and treat him as my own child."

In 1809 Charbonneau and Sacagawea took Jean Baptiste to St. Louis. There Charbonneau received his promised land warrant for 320 acres (129 hectares) and $533.33 for his services as interpreter. This was a small fortune to a man of limited economic resources. On March 26, 1811, Charbonneau sold his land to Clark for $100. The old trapper and Sacagawea boarded a barge bound for the upper Missouri, leaving Jean Baptiste with Clark to start an education.

Jean Baptiste returned west after completing his schooling. In 1823 at age eighteen, he met Prince Paul Wilhelm of Wurttemberg, Germany, who was on a scientific mission to the United States. Jean Baptiste's unusual combination of frontier skills and culture intrigued the prince, who took him to Europe. For six years, Jean Baptiste enjoyed a royal lifestyle. He became fluent in four languages.

Jean Baptiste returned to the United States in 1829 and ranged throughout the West, hunting, trapping, guiding, and exploring. In 1847, he was appointed *alcalde* (mayor) of San Luis Rey Mission, which is preserved in modern-day Oceanside, California. He later joined the gold rush in northern California and next appeared in 1861 as a hotel clerk in Auburn, California.

Five years later, the sixty-one-year-old adventurer left Auburn with two companions and headed toward new gold discoveries in Montana. On the way, Jean Baptiste got pneumonia and died. He was buried in a remote, primitive cemetery in the tiny hamlet of Danner, Oregon. On March 14, 1973, Jean Baptiste's grave was entered into the National Register of Historic Places.

paddling upriver and learned that Vice President Aaron Burr had killed Alexander Hamilton in a duel and that the Spanish and the British had fired on U.S. ships.

Meeting former army acquaintances, Clark wrote that they were "Somewhat astonished to see us return and appeared rejoiced to meet us." Apparently, the Corps had been "Long Since given out by the people of the US Generaly and almost forgotten...," although "the President of the U. States had yet hopes of us." So in the end, it was Jefferson who still believed in them

The men paddled frantically toward St. Louis, where their heroic adventure ended on September 23, 1806.

CHAPTER 8
AFTERMATH AND EVENTUALITIES

The Corps of Discovery was welcomed home with jubilation. The men were heroes, but their work was not done. The captains still had to report to Jefferson.

In St. Louis, the Corps disbanded. Congress awarded Lewis and Clark 1,600 acres (647 hectares) of land each, in addition to their regular pay. The enlisted men received double pay and 320 acres (129 hectares) of land as reward for their services. "Now," wrote John Ordway, the young and responsible sergeant from New Hampshire, "we intend to return to our native homes to see our parents once more, as we have been so long from them."

The captains traveled to Washington. Dances and parties were held in their honor in the towns they passed through. At the capital, one senator told Lewis it was as if he had just returned from the moon!

The story of the expedition does not end well for Jefferson's friend Meriwether Lewis. Appointed governor of the Louisiana Territory, he found the duties a burden, and politics and bureaucracy soon overwhelmed the young farmer and explorer.

A government clerk accused him of squandering money when dealing with the Indians. The charges involved several minor expenditures required to return Mandan Chief Big White to his tribe after his Washington visit. Lewis began to drink, and this aggravated his natural tendency to gloominess. Lewis's sometimes negative feelings about himself can be seen in his lament on his thirty-first birthday—while leading the Corps west over the Bitterroot Mountains—that his life so far had been meaningless, and that he must rededicate himself to learning and hard work!

WHAT HAPPENED TO SACAGAWEA AND YORK?

Two additional members of the Corps of Discovery—Sacagawea and York—have been widely acclaimed. Despite their hard work and important contributions during the journey, their status—York as a slave and Sacagawea as Charbonneau's wife—prevented them from improving their lives after the expedition ended.

Sacagawea returned with her husband to the Mandan villages in 1811. There she gave birth to a daughter named Lisette. She apparently died of a fever in 1812 at Fort Manuel, a fur-trading post. The fort site has been flooded by Lake Oahe, but a monument honoring Sacagawea can be found along U.S. Highway 12 near Mobridge, South Dakota. Interestingly, a second grave for Sacagawea is located on the Wind River Reservation in Wyoming. An elderly Indian woman who died on the reservation in 1884 was reported to be the Sacagawea of Corps of Discovery fame, but most historians dispute this story.

In recent years, Sacagawea became well known when her likeness was used on a new U.S. "golden dollar" coin that was introduced in 2000. By all accounts, she was a popular choice, but the coin was a flop—U.S. citizens do not like to carry and use dollar coins—and minting was halted in 2002.

William Clark's slave York was rarely mentioned in expedition journals, but he was an intriguing member of the Corps. The color of his skin made him a slave to the whites, but York also played a valuable role in impressing Indians, who thought that he must be a great warrior because he was black. He often carried a rifle and was genuinely attached to Clark, with whom he grew up in Kentucky.

When the Corps disbanded in St. Louis, York asked Clark for his freedom, in part because he wanted to live near his wife, a slave in Kentucky. Clark refused. As a result, the captain noted that York sulked and "became difficult." In a letter discussing the matter, Meriwether Lewis counseled harsh measures. Clark took his advice and rented York to a man who apparently abused him. Upon his return to Clark, York was so "insolent and sulky" that Clark beat him.

Many years after the expedition—possibly in 1816 or later—Clark finally gave York his freedom. Apparently, he also gave him a horse and wagon and helped him start a freight-hauling business. Competing with white freight haulers in the climate of the time, however, was difficult, and York's business failed. He died in 1832, possibly of cholera, in Tennessee.

Lewis apparently fell into a deep depression. He took no action to rewrite his field notes or edit his journals. Perhaps the perfect explorer and leader, Lewis was not the perfect civil servant. On October 11, 1809, while traveling to Washington to defend himself against charges of mismanagement, he shot himself. Some people thought he must have been murdered, but Clark and Jefferson, who understood Lewis and his dark moods, knew it was suicide.

Clark's years were longer and happier. He married and raised a brood of children, including Jean Baptiste, his adored "Pompey." Appointed general of the Louisiana

A monument in City Park, Portland, Oregon, to Sacagawea

territorial militia and superintendent of Indian affairs for the territory, Clark cultivated the friendship and trust of the Indians during terribly trying times. He named his first son after his friend, Meriwether Lewis Clark.

Results

Did the Corps of Discovery accomplish Thomas Jefferson's objectives? White traders and trappers were probably unaffected by its trek and discoveries since private adventurers had already headed west before the Corps was organized. The Corps did not find a "direct & practicable water communication across this continent." Lewis took this failure to find the "Northwest Passage" personally, unaware that there was none to find. Native Americans already knew about the many species of plants, animals, and birds carefully observed and described for the first time in Corps journals. The captains neglected to complete their journals for publication. While Sergeant Patrick Gass published his field notes promptly, the two captains' voluminous journals trickled into print gradually.

Native Americans can argue that the Corps journey did not represent a high point in their history. The Corps enjoyed good relations with most of the tribes it encountered, but they returned from the expedition with their views of Native Americans as primitive people little changed. The successful completion of the expedition encouraged more people to turn their attention to the West, and soon there was a flood of white Americans onto Native land. Not surprisingly, the United States spent much of the nineteenth century at war with Native American tribes in the West.

As a symbolic achievement, however, the journey of the Corps of Discovery was crucial to knitting the land between the Atlantic and Pacific oceans into one nation. Other land purchases, military conquests, and international treaties followed that would extend the borders of the United States to the Rio Grande in the south, to the Pacific coast of California in the west, and even to Alaska in the north.

On a personal scale, the physical journey of the Corps was magnificent. News of the accomplishment electrified the United States in 1806. The leadership of Lewis and Clark and the endurance of the exploring party were heroic, and thus the spirit of the Corps will continue to inspire generations of men and women.

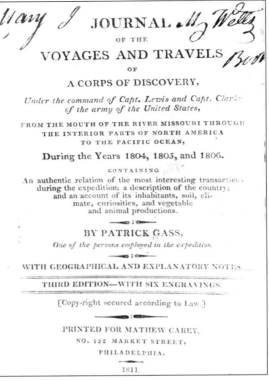

The title page from the *Journal of the Voyages and Travels of a Corps of Discovery* by Patrick Gass, published in 1811. This book described the Lewis and Clark expedition of 1804–1806 into the Louisiana Purchase territory.

Rose Anne Abrahamson (*left*) of the Lehmi Shoshone tribe and Amy Mossett (*center*) of the Mandan-Hidatsa-Arikara Nation hold the plaque naming Native American Sacagawea honorary scout of the Corps of Discovery. President Bill Clinton applauds after presenting it to them in the East Room of the White House on January 17, 2001.

Places to Visit and Research

Many sites crucial to Meriwether Lewis, William Clark, and the Corps of Discovery can be researched online or visited. Below is a list, in alphabetical order, of those historic sites, parks, and museums, along with their addresses, telephone numbers, and Web sites. Places described in the sidebars are shown on the map on page 59 with green dots. The red dots refer to other places important to the Lewis and Clark expedition.

1 Bitterroot National Forest
1801 North 1st Street, Hamilton, MT 59840. (406) 363-7117.
www.fs.fed.us/r1/bitterroot
The online brochure at www.fs.fed.us/r1/bitterroot/heritage/landc/lewis_clark.pdf provides information on retracing parts of the Corps's route through the Bitterroots. See page 41.

2 Cape Disappointment State Park/Lewis and Clark Interpretive Center
P.O. Box 488, Ilwaco, WA 98624. (360) 642-3029. www.parks.wa.gov/lewisandclark/lcinterpctr.asp. See page 45.

3 Fort Union Trading Post National Historic Site
15550 Hwy. 1804, Williston, ND 58801. (701) 572-9083
www.nps.gov/fous
Located at the confluence of Yellowstone and Missouri rivers, this restored trading post tells the story of the flourishing nineteenth-century fur trade.

4 Giant Springs State Park
4600 Giant Springs Road, Great Falls, MT 59405. (406) 454-5840. fwp.state.mt.us/parks/lewisclark/visit/default.html
Freshwater spring discovered by Lewis and Clark. The park now features a fish hatchery and nature hikes.

5 Jefferson National Expansion Memorial
11 North 4th St., St. Louis, MO 63102. (314) 421-1023. www.nps.gov/jeff/index.html. See page 19

6 Joslyn Art Museum
2200 Dodge Street, Omaha, NE 68102-1292. (402) 342-3300. www.joslyn.org
This museum, located just blocks from the Missouri River, features the work of artists who traveled and painted scenes along the route of the Corps of Discovery in the 1800s.

7 Katy Trail State Park and Tavern Cave
P.O. Box 176, Jefferson City, MO 65102. (660) 882-8196. www.katytrailstatepark.com
This 225-mile biking and hiking trail roughly follows the Missouri River across the state. West of St. Charles it passes the 300-foot-high bluff off which Meriwether Lewis nearly fell.

8 Knife River Indian Villages National Historic Site
P.O. Box 9, Stanton, ND 58571-0009. (701) 745-3300.
www.nps.gov/knri
The site features earth lodges and cultural artifacts of the Hidatsa and Mandan.

9 Lewis & Clark Center
701 Riverside Dr., St. Charles, MO 63301. (314) 947-3199. www.lewisandclarktrail.com
Dioramas tell the story of the Corps of Discovery. See page 28.

10 Lewis and Clark Interpretive Center/Sergeant Floyd Monument
900 Larsen Park Road, Sioux City, IA 51102. (712) 224-5242. www.siouxcitylcic.com. See page 29.

11 Lewis and Clark National Historic Trail
1709 Jackson Street, Omaha, NE 68102. (402) 514-9311. www.nps.gov/lecl
The National Park Service does not own any section of Lewis and Clark Trail, but this office provides oversight and coordination.

12 Historic Trail Interpretive Center
P.O. Box 1806, 4201 Giant Springs Road, Great Falls, MT 59403-1806. (407) 727-8733. www.fs.fed.us/r1/lewisclark/lcic. See pages 12 and 39.

13 Lewis & Clark State Historic Site/Camp Dubois
One Lewis and Clark Trail, Hartford, IL 62048. (618) 251-5811. www.campdubois.com. See page 26.

14 Lewis and Clark National Historical Parks
92343 Fort Clatsop Road, Astoria, OR 97103-9197. (503) 861-2471, ext. 214. www.nps.gov/focl. See page 47.

15 Lewis and Clark State Park
21914 Park Loop, Onawa, IA 51040. (712) 423-2829. www.iowadnr.com/parks/state_park_list/lewis_clark.html
This park, site of a Corps camp in August 1804, features a display with replicas of a keelboat and pirogues used on the expedition. See page 27.

16 Little Bighorn Battlefield
P.O. Box 39, Crow Agency, MT 59022. (406) 638-3204. www.nps.gov/libi. See page 51.

17 Missouri National Recreational River
P.O. Box 591, O'Neill, NE 68763. (402) 336-3970. www.nps.gov/mnrr
This long, scenic stretch of river has not changed much since Lewis and Clark's time. It features the Lewis and Clark Visitor Center.

18 Monticello/The Thomas Jefferson Foundation
P.O. Box 217, Charlottesville, VA 22902. (434) 984-9800. www.monticello.org. See page 9.

19 Museum of the Mountain Man
700 E. Hennick, Pinedale, WY 82941. (877) 686-6266.www.museumofthemountainman.com. See page 13.

20 North Dakota Lewis and Clark Interpretive Center/Fort Mandan
P.O. Box 607/US Hwy 83 & ND Hwy. 200A, Washburn, ND 58577-0607. (701) 402-8535 www.fortmandan.com. See page 35.

21 Pompeys Pillar National Monument
Pompeys Pillar Historical Assn., P.O. Box 227, Worden, MT 59088. (406) 875-2233. www.pompeyspillar.org. See page 51.

22 River's Edge Trail
P.O. Box 553, Great Falls, MT 59403. (406) 788-3313. www.thetrail.org
This 25-mile (40-kilometer) trail connects parks, waterfalls, dams, and points of interest in the vicinity of the Corps' epic portage around the Great Falls of the Missouri.

23 Sacajawea State Park & Interpretative Center
2503 Sacajawea Park Road, Pasco, WA 99301.(360) 902-8844. www.parks.wa.gov/lewisandclark/lcsacainterpctr.asp. See page 43.

24 San Luis Rey Mission
4050 Mission Avenue, Oceanside, CA 92057. (760) 757-4613. www.sanluisrey.org.
Sacagawea's son governed this mission.

25 Upper Missouri River Breaks National Monument
P.O. Box 1160, Lewiston, MT 59457. (406) 538-7461. www.mt.blm.gov. See page 36.

This map shows the location of the sites identified in the Places to Visit and Research section. Those sites shown in green are also mentioned in sidebars.

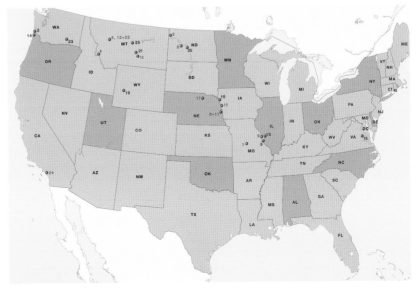

Time Line

1792
Sea captain Robert Gray discovers Columbia River.

1799
Meriwether Lewis serves in army under William Clark.

1800
France acquires New Orleans and Louisiana Territories. Thomas Jefferson elected president.

1801
Lewis becomes Jefferson's secretary.

1802
Jefferson asks Lewis to command expedition.

1803
January Jefferson asks Congress for $2,500 for a "commercial expedition."
June Lewis chooses Clark as co-leader. Scientists tutor Lewis.
July Napoleon sells New Orleans and Louisiana Territories to U.S. for $15 million.
October Lewis's group travels over falls of Ohio River.

1804
May Corps departs Camp Wood (Camp Dubois), Illinois.
August Sergeant Charles Floyd dies on the 20th.
September Corps views "immense herds" of buffalo, elk, deer, antelope and wolves. The men struggled with mosquitoes, sunstroke, and prickly pear cactus. They were harassed by Teton Sioux.

October Corps reaches Mandan and Hidatsa villages.
November Corps begins building Fort Mandan. Jefferson reelected president.

1805
Winter Toussaint Charbonneau and George Drouillard join as interpreters. Sacagawea gives birth to "Pompey."
April Captains send collection of flora and fauna to Jefferson. Corps departs Fort Mandan.
June Corps reaches Marias River and spends one week exploring and discussing directions. Corps spends one month portaging around Great Falls.
August Lewis sees ranges of snow-covered mountains in the distance. Meet Shoshone. Sacagawea reunited with brother. Corps climbs into mountains.
September Heavy snow falls. Starving Corps kills and eats horses. Meet Nez Perce. Subsist on fish and roots.
October Corps portages around rapids on Columbia River and encounters many native peoples.
November Corps reaches Pacific Ocean at "Cape Disappointment" and vote to make winter quarters on south bank of Columbia.
December Fort Clatsop completed.

1806
March Corps departs Fort Clatsop.
May With the Nez Perce, wait for snows to melt.
June Advance into mountains.

July Corps splits. Clark follows Yellowstone River and Sacagawea guides him through Bozeman Pass. Crow warriors steal horses. Clark carves his name and date on "Pompeys Pillar." Lewis travels north, searching for shortcut to upper Missouri and encounters hostile Blackfeet.
August Corps reunites. Charbonneau, Sacagawea, and Jean Baptiste depart at Mandan villages.
September Corps returns to St. Louis on the 23rd.

1807
Lewis appointed governor of Louisiana Territory. Clark appointed general of militia and superintendent of Indian Affairs in new territories.

1809
Jefferson's second term ends. Lewis dies from gunshot wounds, perhaps self-inflicted.

1813
Clark appointed governor of Missouri Territory.

1814
Lewis and Clark journals published.

1838
William Clark dies.

Glossary

Barracks
A building used to house soldiers in a fort or other military installation

Beaver
A dam-building, water-loving mammal with luxurious fur that was prized for making clothing. Trappers pursued this common animal across North America, and a flourishing trade for its pelts developed from the 1600s through the early 1800s.

Bison
A large, hoofed animal that roamed the plains of North America in huge herds at the time of Lewis and Clark. Also called *buffalo*.

Bitterroots
Rugged mountain range running from north to south in Idaho and Montana

Bow
A flexible stick of wood bent by string tied at both ends. Designed to shoot arrows for hunting and war.

Cache
A hiding place for clothing, ammunition, or other items of value

Camas root
A flowering plant, native to the Pacific Northwest, whose roots were used as food by Native American tribes. Though nutritious, the roots are poisonous unless cooked; members of the Corps became sick after eating camas root.

Canoe
A slender boat with a light frame covered by skins or bark. Tapered at both ends, it is paddled by hand.

Columbia River
The major river system in the Pacific Northwest. The main river originates in Canada, crosses into the U.S., then turns west.

Confluence
The place where two rivers join together

Continental Divide
The imaginary line running from north to south through western North America (roughly along the Rocky Mountains) and separates the watersheds of the two oceans that border the continent. Water to the west of the divide flows to the Pacific and water to the east flows to the Atlantic.

Flintlock
A shoulder-held firearm in which flint strikes steel, producing a spark that ignites gunpowder and fires a lead ball

Journal
A personal written record of daily events, experiences, and ideas

Louisiana Purchase
More than 828,000 square miles (2.14 million square kilometers) of land purchased by the United States from France in 1803 for $15 million. The territory covered the drainage of the Mississippi River from the river west to the Rocky Mountains.

Missouri River
The longest river in North America and the route that the Corps generally followed east of the Continental Divide on both legs of its journey. The river rises in Montana's Rocky Mountains and flows in a southeasterly direction to St. Louis on the Mississippi River.

Musket
A heavy, slow-to-load, shoulder-fired gun that is generally inaccurate beyond 100 yards (91 meters). The inside of the barrel is smooth, in comparison to a rifle, which has a grooved barrel that gives fired bullets a twist and makes them more accurate.

Northwest Passage
Fabled route between the Atlantic and Pacific oceans that many thought would allow easier trade between the Orient and Europe. Finding this route was an important goal of the Lewis and Clark expedition.

Palisade
An enclosed fence constructed of tall, wooden stakes usually built for defensive purposes

Pirogue
A type of canoe that may be as simple as a boat fashioned from a log—a "dugout"—or a large and elaborately fashioned canoe for hauling people and freight

Portage
Carrying a boat and its contents over land to avoid an obstacle in the water

Rendezvous
A prearranged meeting for the purpose of conducting business. In the West, trappers, traders, and Native Americans would meet, usually once per year, to exchange furs and other goods.

Salmon
A highly prized fish eaten by Indians of the Pacific Northwest

Slave
A person who is the property of, and whose life and actions are controlled by, another person

Trade
Bartering items of value, usually without the exchange of money

Further Resources

Books

Adler, David, and Dan Brown (illus.), *A Picture Book of Sacagawea*, New York: Holiday House, 2003

Adler, David, and Ronald Himler (illus.), *A Picture Book of Lewis and Clark*, New York: Holiday House, 2003

Ambrose, Stephen E., *This Vast Land: A Young Man's Journal of the Lewis and Clark Expedition*. Waterville, ME: Thorndike Press, 2004.

Bowen, Andy Russell, *The Back of Beyond: A Story about Lewis and Clark*. Minneapolis, MN: Carolrhoda Books, 1997.

Bebenroth, Charlotta M., *Meriwether Lewis, Boy Explorer*. New York: Aladdin Paperbacks, 1997.

Blumberg, Rhoda, *York's Adventures with Lewis and Clark: An African-American's Part in the Great Expedition*, New York: HarperCollins, 2004

Bruchac, Joseph, *Sacajawea: The Story of Bird Woman and the Lewis and Clark Expedition*. San Diego, CA: Silver Whistle, 2000.

Faber, Harold, *Lewis and Clark: From Ocean to Ocean*. New York: Benchmark Books, 2002.

Feinstein, Stephen, *Read about Sacagawea*. Berkeley Heights, NJ: Enslow Publishers, 2004.

Fradin, Dennis B., *Who was Sacagawea?* New York: Grosset & Dunlap, 2002.

Hamilton, John, *The Missouri River*. Edina, MN: ABDO & Daughters, 2003.

Herbert, Janis, *Lewis and Clark for Kids: Their Journey of Discovery with 21 Activities*, Chicago: Chicago Review Press, 2000

Johmann, Carol A., *The Lewis & Clark Expedition: Join the Corps of Discovery to Explore Uncharted Territory*. Charlotte, VT: Williamson Pub., 2003.

Kimmel, Elizabeth Cody, *As Far as the Eye Can Reach: Lewis and Clark's Westward Quest*. New York: Landmark Books/Random House, 2003.

Lourie, Peter, *On the Trail of Lewis and Clark: A Journey up the Missouri*. Honesdale, PA: Boyds Mills Press, 2004.

Maynard, Charles W. (Charles William), *Fort Clatsop*. New York: PowerKids Press, 2002.

Milton, Joyce, *Sacajawea: Her True Story*. New York: Grosset & Dunlap, 2001.

Molzahn, Arlene Bourgeois, *Lewis and Clark: American Explorers*. Berkeley Heights, NJ : Enslow Publishers, 2003.

Orr, Tamra, *The Lewis and Clark Expedition: A Primary Source History of the Journey of the Corps of Discovery*, New York: The Rosen Publishing Group, 2004

Patent, Dorothy Hinshaw, *Animals on the Trail with Lewis and Clark*. New York: Clarion Books, 2002.

Patent, Dorothy Hinshaw, *The Lewis and Clark Trail: Then and Now*. New York: Dutton Children's Books, 2002.

Redmond, Shirley-Raye, Lewis and Clark: *A Prairie Dog for the President*. New York: Random House, 2003.

Rodger, Ellen, *Lewis and Clark: Opening the American West*. New York: Crabtree, 2005.

Sanford, William R. (William Reynolds), *Sacagawea: Native American Hero*. Springfield, NJ: Enslow Publishers, 1997.

Schanzer, Rosalyn, *How We Crossed the West: The Adventures of Lewis & Clark*. Washington, D.C.: National Geographic Society, 1997.

Stein, Conrad, *Lewis and Clark*, Chicago: Children's Press, 1997

Waller, Rosemary, *Sacagawea 1788-1812*, Mankato, Minn.: Blue Earth Books (Capstone Press), 2003

Web Sites

Discovering Lewis & Clark
www.lewis-clark.org

Lewis & Clark Mapping the West
www.edgate.com/lewisandclark

Lewis & Clark National Historic Trail
www.nps.gov/lecl

Lewis & Clark—PBS
www.pbs.org/lewisandclark

Lewis and Clark Trail Heritage Foundation
www.lewisandclark.org

Lewis & Clark's Historic Trail
www.lewisclark.net

LewisAndClarkTrail.com
lewisandclarktrail.com

National Geographic: Lewis & Clark
www.nationalgeographic.com/lewisandclark

National Lewis & Clark Bicentennial Commemoration
www.lewisandclark200.org

Index